AUG 8 2003

VEHICLE MAINTENANCE TIPS FOR THE AVERAGE GUY (OR GIRL)

BY

MARC R. WILLIAMS

© 2001 by Marc R. Williams. All rights reserved.

No part of this book may be reproduced, stored in a retrieval system, or transmitted by any means, electronic, mechanical, photocopying, recording, or otherwise, without written permission from the author.

ISBN: 0-7596-5866-8

This book is printed on acid free paper.

1st books rev 7/30/01

Vehicle Information

Make: ____________

Model: ____________

Year: ____________

Color: ____________

VIN: ____________

Insurance Co.: ____________

____

Policy Number: ____________

TABLE OF CONTENTS

DISCLAIMER

The author assumes no liability for any damage, or catastrophe, that might occur from the use of information found in this manual. This manual, like all others, could contain a typographical error or other mis-quotation, so it never hurts to double check or get a second opinion when in doubt. I did the best I could to keep it factual, informative, and hopefully even a bit entertaining. Please be careful as you venture under the hood. There are many strange things there that can burn, cut, bruise, or otherwise abuse you!

INTRODUCTION

Hi! I am Marc R. Williams. Let me tell you a little bit about myself. (In other words what qualifies me to write this manual?) For the better part of my life I have used machinery of some type or other, everything from lawnmowers as a child to cars, trucks, airplanes, and everything in between as an adult. When I first started mowing the lawn as a child of five or six I didn't know squat about oil or other aspects of maintenance. I soon ran dads old mower low on oil. He hadn't told me about that and one day he asked me about the oil level in the engine. I could only shrug and give him dumb looks. We checked the oil together and found that although the level was a bit low no damage had been done. We changed the oil and put the mower back to work, this time a lot more safely. This was my first lesson with regards to operating machinery. I never forgot it!

As time went on I found I had a knack for tuning and then later building engines and doing most anything with a vehicle I needed to do. I really couldn't find anyone who could do what I wanted to a car, the way I wanted, and not try to rip me off. So I learned to do it myself. Now to be sure, <u>NO</u> technician knows it all (myself included) and if you hear one say he knows it all just smile sympathetically and walk away. You would be walking away from an idiot!

I started out reading every book or manual I could get my hands on pertaining to the particular vehicle or situation I was involved with. Then I would test what I had found to see if it would work (books are not always 100% right). With much testing and trial and error I became more and more capable with these vehicles and soon enough I had hooked up with a local automobile dealership. This resulted in much valuable factory training. I eventually got into other things but continued to build vehicles for my personal use and occasionally for others. During this time ONE KEY FACT stared me in the face constantly. The best, most expensive vehicle made isn't gonna cut it without that one thing- PROPER MAINTENANCE!

PROPER MAINTENANCE

Over the years I began to notice friends, acquaintances, heck even people I didn't know were asking me many questions about oil, fuel, anti-freeze, what to use, when to use it, and how often. This gave me the idea to put my ideas, beliefs, and some experiences in this manual. I hope it helps you in some way! No doubt you will end up with a safer, better performing, and longer lasting vehicle. As much as we use our vehicles it's the least we can do for them. Thanks for purchasing this manual!

Hey Marc, what kind of oil should I use in my car? How many times have I been asked that one? Now don't get me wrong, I don't mind people asking me that. Indeed it was me asking that question some years ago. We've all got to start somewhere. My answer is if you stay with a major brand there isn't a bad oil. I have my personal preference but I am not on the payroll of any petroleum refiner/distributor so I will not refer to brand names. I have not seen a failure directly related to the type of oil used. Only if the oil was not changed often enough or the wrong viscosity was used. In the event of a lack of maintenance any oil will eventually break down and lose its ability to properly lubricate and protect parts. Eventually most any oil will turn to sludge. This is such a tragedy and so unnecessary. I change my oil in my daily driver at 2,500 miles or less. Even more frequently on my high-performers or any vehicle subjected to rough conditions such as stop and go traffic, short trips, dusty conditions, excessive heat or cold, (thats right, in some cold climates, vehicles with cooling systems that perform well in the summer may not get their engines hot enough in the winter to burn out the water condensation that occurs in every engine. This water eventually turns into a type of acid- something you don't want in your engine. All these factors can require a more frequent oil/filter change. I have heard of cases in which some people do a lot of long distance driving and changed their oil at extended intervals such as 3,000 to 5,000 miles. I personally don't care for that but under no circumstance would I go beyond that mileage on one oil change period. I run my engines hard, they are not cheap at any rate so I prefer that they be full of good clean oil. Remember oil doesn't just lubricate, it also cools the engine (it draws heat away from the parts as it lubricates them.) So I run my engines at the proper level, adding oil a few ounces at a time if necessary to keep it max full.

VEHICLE MAINTENANCE TIPS

List of important part numbers

Name	Part Number	Qty. Used
Oil Filter		
Fuel Filter		
Air Filter		
Fan Belt		
Alternator Belt		
Power Steering Belt		
Air Conditioner Belt		
Top Radiator Hose		
Bottom Radiator Hose		
Heater Hose Size		
Tire Size		
Wiper Blades		

VEHICLE MAINTENANCE TIPS

Service Interval Chart

Date	Mileage	Type Svc.

VEHICLE MAINTENANCE TIPS

Service Interval Chart

Date	Mileage	Type Svc.

VEHICLE MAINTENANCE TIPS

Service Interval Chart

Date	Mileage	Type Svc.

VEHICLE MAINTENANCE TIPS

Service Interval Chart

Date	Mileage	Type Svc.

VEHICLE MAINTENANCE TIPS

Service Interval Chart

Date	Mileage	Type Svc.

VEHICLE MAINTENANCE TIPS

Service Interval Chart

Date	Mileage	Type Svc.

VEHICLE MAINTENANCE TIPS

Service Interval Chart

Date	Mileage	Type Svc.

VEHICLE MAINTENANCE TIPS

Service Interval Chart

Date	Mileage	Type Svc.

VEHICLE MAINTENANCE TIPS

Service Interval Chart

Date	Mileage	Type Svc.

VEHICLE MAINTENANCE TIPS

Service Interval Chart

Date	Mileage	Type Svc.

OIL VISCOSITY

What about viscosity? Most vehicle manufacturers list oils (viscosities) that are appropriate for the conditions under which the owner expects to use the vehicle. For instance, someone in Florida in the summer might want a bit thicker oil than someone in Alaska in the winter. Oil with a lower viscosity flows more quickly when cold and therefore gets to the parts faster. It is well known that most of an engines wear comes as a result of cold starts. A low viscosity oil also is easier for an engine to pump and flows more freely in general resulting in less fuel consumption and more power. Consequently in recent years most oil manufacturers have come up with 5W/30 oils and there's even a 0W/30.

I might use them in the winter in a cold climate but in the summer or in a warmer climate I feel uncomfortable with anything thinner than a 10W/30. Older engines with more wear can sometimes benefit from the use of a thicker oil such as a 10W/40, or a 20W/50 or similar oils. There are some single viscosity oils such as 20, 30, 40, 50, and 60 weights. There are actually oils thinner and thicker in a single weight but they tend to be a bit hard to find. Theoretically a 30 weight oil is supposed to be exactly the same when warm as a 10W/30 when warm. I have found the straight 30 to be perhaps a hair thicker at the same temp. Such has been my experience when comparing say a 10W/40 to a straight 40, or a 20W/50 to a straight 50.

DIESEL ENGINES

How about a diesel? A diesel engine does its job by having higher compression of the air in its cylinders resulting in a combustion temperature hot enough that when fuel is injected into the cylinder at just the right moment this hot temp ignites the mixture- so there is no distributor, no spark plugs. At the same time this higher compression causes more gasses to escape past the pistons into the crankcase below. The result? These gasses contaminate the oil much more quickly than in a gasoline engine. So the diesel would need at least as frequent an oil change as a gas engine but preferably more often. Some years back when I worked for an oil change company I had a trick I used to show the customers with diesels. I would change the oil and filter, make sure the engine had the proper level of oil, start the engine, check for leaks, then immediately shut the engine off. I would then pull the dipstick and show the customer the oil. It would be as dark as the oil that came out! No it wasn't as dirty or as worn out but this trick simply illustrated just how fast a diesel would contaminate its new oil. I like a diesel, don't get me wrong. You just gotta pay attention to its unique requirements. Can a diesel use the same oil as a gas engine? Yes, for the most part this is true if you use a quality oil of the proper viscosity. However, most oil companies have oils specially formulated for diesels. These oils are available in a variety of viscosities but the one I see most often is a 15W/40. (Remember, with its higher compression, a diesel is harder to start, a thicker oil that might benefit it when it was warm would make starting that much more difficult) in my own diesels I would use the 15W/40 diesel oil with confidence. You can also use the 'diesel' oils in a gas engine. If it cost a heck of a lot more I don't believe I would do it. The existing oils for gas engines are more than adequate.

VEHICLE MAINTENANCE TIPS

List of important part numbers

Name	Part Number	Qty. Used
Oil Filter		
Fuel Filter		
Air Filter		
Fan Belt		
Alternator Belt		
Power Steering Belt		
Air Conditioner Belt		
Top Radiator Hose		
Bottom Radiator Hose		
Heater Hose Size		
Tire Size		
Wiper Blades		

VEHICLE MAINTENANCE TIPS

Service Interval Chart

Date	Mileage	Type Svc.

VEHICLE MAINTENANCE TIPS

Service Interval Chart

Date	Mileage	Type Svc.

VEHICLE MAINTENANCE TIPS

Service Interval Chart

Date	Mileage	Type Svc.

VEHICLE MAINTENANCE TIPS

Service Interval Chart

Date	Mileage	Type Svc.

VEHICLE MAINTENANCE TIPS

Service Interval Chart

Date	Mileage	Type Svc.

VEHICLE MAINTENANCE TIPS

Service Interval Chart

Date	Mileage	Type Svc.

VEHICLE MAINTENANCE TIPS

Service Interval Chart

Date	Mileage	Type Svc.

VEHICLE MAINTENANCE TIPS

Service Interval Chart

Date	Mileage	Type Svc.

VEHICLE MAINTENANCE TIPS

Service Interval Chart

Date	Mileage	Type Svc.

VEHICLE MAINTENANCE TIPS

Service Interval Chart

Date	Mileage	Type Svc.

MOTORCYCLES

How about motorcycles and other small engines? Most motorcycle and small engine manufacturers are very specific about the oil requirements of their products. I would check with the dealer or the owners manual but at any rate I would service them more often than a larger, slower running vehicle. In most cases the amount of oil required is much less and also in many cases as in lawnmowers, tillers, snow blowers ETC there is no odometer, you must service them at time intervals rather than mileage. Good judgement, common sense, and the fact that it is better to over-maintain than to undermaintain should prevail here. Furthermore many small engines are 2-cycle engines, meaning oil is mixed with the fuel prior to combustion either manually, or automatically. Specifically calibrated oils are required for 2-cycle engines and highly recommended. Conventional motor oil can be used in a two stroke (2-cycle) engine but only, <u>ONLY</u>, in an emergency. Otherwise gumming of the fuel system and severe carboning up of the combustion chamber will result. Don't do it unless life or limb depends on it, get enough to last you while you are getting so you wont be tempted to 'cheat'.

To use synthetic or not to, is that the question? (Sorry, Bill Shakespeare) This is another question I have been asked many times. Synthetic oils, like all other things automotive, had to prove to me they were better before I would use them. When they first appeared on the scene I was a bit skeptical. I continued to use conventional oil which I knew could cut it. In due time, however, I saw things that impressed me. First, I noticed a lot of long distance race cars were using it quite successfully. Then I heard a story about a major automotive manufacturer that was having a problem with its flagship sportscar. It seems one of its cam bearings was galding. No doubt it was one of the cam bearings farthest away from the oil pump. The oil residue that remained on the bearing wasn't enough to protect it during cold start up, and the oil being pumped by the oil pump wasn't getting there fast enough to protect the bearing. So it would gald. The company fixed the problem by switching the engine over to synthetic. That was all it took! The oil residue that remained behind lubricated the bearing better during cold start then the synthetic oil flowed to the bearing much faster than the conventional oil did. Voila', problem solved. Impressive! Some time later I saw an engine that was being tested on a dynomometer (a device that determines the horsepower output of the engine) which had in it conventional oil. The power output at this point was 398 horsepower. The oil and filter were then changed and this time synthetic was added. No other changes were made at this time! The engine was fired up and retested. Output now? 418 horsepower! I was convinced! I tried it in my own engines and liked it. Now all my engines have synthetic inside them, even the lawnmower! As far as I am concerned there are only three scenarios where synthetic shouldn't be used. One, if you have an old, high mileage engine that has been running on conventional oil leave it be. Don't swap it over at this point. Two, when I go to break in a new engine I prefer to do so with conventional oil. For instance if I am using 'Brand X' conventional oil and I have a fresh engine to break in I will install the

'Brand X' conventional oil, break the engine in wide open, drain the oil, remove the old filter, install the new filter and 'Brand X' synthetic oil then down the road I go. note: I said I break in the engine wide open-this is something which flies in the face of conventional wisdom, but all my engines are high performance engines, I run 'em hard, I break 'em in hard. I have enjoyed fantastic success with this method. If you are not comfortable with this thats OK, go with your own heart in this matter, the main point is even though most synthetic oil manufacturers say it's OK to break in a new engine with synthetic I prefer not to. (Synthetic is so much slicker I am concerned it might take the rings longer to seat or they might not ever seat at all.) This brings up the third scenario where I would not use synthetic. Most manufacturers of camshafts and valve lifters recommend against breaking in new cams and lifters with synthetic oil. Even if I had an engine that had been running for some time on synthetic and I needed to install a new camshaft and new lifters, I would revert back to same brand conventional oil for the duration of the break in period then return to synthetic.

VEHICLE MAINTENANCE TIPS

Service Interval Chart

Date	Mileage	Type Svc.

VEHICLE MAINTENANCE TIPS

Service Interval Chart

Date	Mileage	Type Svc.

VEHICLE MAINTENANCE TIPS

Service Interval Chart

Date	Mileage	Type Svc.

VEHICLE MAINTENANCE TIPS

Service Interval Chart

Date	Mileage	Type Svc.

VEHICLE MAINTENANCE TIPS

Service Interval Chart

Date	Mileage	Type Svc.

VEHICLE MAINTENANCE TIPS

Service Interval Chart

Date	Mileage	Type Svc.

VEHICLE MAINTENANCE TIPS

Service Interval Chart

Date	Mileage	Type Svc.

VEHICLE MAINTENANCE TIPS

Service Interval Chart

Date	Mileage	Type Svc.

VEHICLE MAINTENANCE TIPS

Service Interval Chart

Date	Mileage	Type Svc.

VEHICLE MAINTENANCE TIPS

Service Interval Chart

Date	Mileage	Type Svc.

A WORD OF CAUTION

If you do your own oil changes (and many people these days are) BE SURE TO DOUBLE CHECK YOUR WORK AS YOU GO! Make sure the drain plug is properly tightened. Check the old oil filter to see if the old gasket came off with the filter. It is very common for the old gasket to stick to the engine block. When a new filter is installed the new gasket is clamped down against the old gasket. Two gaskets butted together in this manner are rarely able to contain the oil pressure of the engine resulting in a rupture at this point, massive oil loss and massive engine damage! Another thing you might want to do to keep from over filling an engine with oil is to install slightly less at first, crank it to check for leaks, let the oil drain down (this might actually take several hours in some cases) then with the vehicle sitting level check the oil level and add as necessary. For example, if I have a vehicle that is perfectly full at four quarts (according to the 'book') I might install 3.5-3.75 quarts at first, run it, let it drain back then add just enough oil to bring it up to the full mark. Also, BE CAREFUL not to burn yourself, and watch out for things like moving fan blades, moving belts ETC. They will bite you!

FUELS

A word about fuels-when it comes to gasoline I prefer to experiment with the major brands until I find one that performs best in my particular vehicle. I prefer premium fucl, have been known to use the middle octane gas-these two have more cleaning additives as a rule. I personally do not care for the low octane fuels. I have on occasion been known to use fuel from convenient stores, car washes ETC. These places sometimes have excellent fuel-it may even be from a major supplier! Here again I would experiment. When it comes to diesel fuel options are much more limited-less variety. Fuel system cleaner/water remover type additives can benefit both gas and diesel vehicles if used properly. Remember, air and fuel filters are critical to the proper performance of both gas and diesel engines. Proper amounts of air and fuel cannot pass through a dirty filter!

DRIVE TRAIN

How about the transmissions? Transmissions (and also differentials, and transfer cases on all wheel drive vehicles) tend to be neglected when compared to engines. All these gearboxes require lubrication and benefit from servicing. Again, as with engines, morc often under rough conditions. Also synthetic oils are available for transmissions (automatic and manual), and gearboxes as well. Follow the manufacturers recommendations. Gearboxes can usually be serviced at any mileage with no dangcr of screwing something up. In some cases a differential might be of the 'limited slip' type, or 'Posi-Traction', there are many names for these differentials that allow both wheels to engage in low traction circumstances rather than just one. In many cases these special differentials require a special lubricant or a conventional lubricant with a special additive. Make sure you are using the right stuff in your particular situation! In the case of automatic transmissions I have always heard that if you have an auto trans with a lot of miles that has never been serviced do not service it. I have seen exceptions to this rule, but all in all I agree with it. Run such a transmission until it needs an overhaul, overhaul it, then put it on a regular service schedule. Schedules vary from make to make, some manufacturers recommend to never service an automatic transmission, I service my automatics at 10,000 mile intervals, MAX! In recent years I have begun to use transmission pans with a built-in drain plug or add a drain plug to the factory pan. In this case I drop the plug when I change my engine oil then refill with fresh fluid. In most cases dropping the drain plug on an automatic transmission requires a refill of only about 3 or 4 quarts. I am a stick shift fan but sometimes a deal on an automatic trans equipped vehicle comes along that is too good to pass up so I have both sticks and automatics. If you have a stick trans that requires Dextron fluid, USE DEXTRON. If it requires conventional gear lube use that. Using the wrong fluid in a transmission can prove disasterous. There is one exception to this rule I will mention for you performance fans who run automatics. Many of the popular American automatics that came from the factory with Dextron fluid in them can be converted after overhaul to Type F. In other words when you overhaul your transmission and re-install it into the vehicle instead of filling it with Dextron fill it with Type F. This usually results in a firmer shift. Right now I have two automatic trannies of the same type. One has Dextron, the other has Type F, both are doing fine. This may not be possible in all circumstances so by all means check with a reputable transmission shop before doing this. KEEP THAT FLUID LEVEL UP! An automatic trans can run a long time when properly maintained but can be fried quickly if run low on fluid! Heat is the number one enemy of an automatic transmission so make sure yours is running at the proper temperature for its purpose. In other words if you haul a lot of heavy loads or pull a lot of trailers in a warm climate you might need to install a larger fluid cooler. Then again if you live in a very cold climate, running the fluid <u>too cool</u> isn't desirable. Again, check with a reputable shop with regards to your particular application.

COOLANT AND ANTIFREEZE

Is anti-freeze that important? Yes it is! Use of a high quality anti-freeze in the right anti-freeze/water ratio is highly recommended. I have seen many an engine crack and become useless for want of an adequate amount of anti-freeze. Anti-freeze/water in the correct ratio also prevents boil-over in the summer. The cooling system parts whether aluminum, iron, brass, copper, steel, plastic, or whatever other materiel you might have are better protected by proper anti-freeze levels. Many manufacturers are claiming extended servicing periods for cooling systems. Some as much as 150,000 miles or more. This may be fine but for myself a bit extended. I have serviced my cooling systems once a year for years, usually just before the winter and I will continue to do so. It is an extra expense but use of distilled water with the anti-freeze can cut down on mineral deposits on the cooling system parts. Also, remember belts, radiator hoses, caps, heater hoses, water pumps, ETC don't go forever. Check for unusual bulges in the hoses, frayed belts, any leaks. I usually change my hoses at a maximum of five year intervals, usually less. I consider a hose bad regardless of age if it has the aforementioned bulge, if it is too soft, or if I rake my thumbnail across it and little chunks of rubber come off. While you are in this area check supplemental fluids- brake fluid, power steering fluid, clutch fluid (if applicable), be sure no dirt falls into the reservoir and make sure all caps are secured properly. Don't Forget the thermostat!

VEHICLE MAINTENANCE TIPS

Antifreeze Service/Belts & Hoses Checked

Date	Mileage	Protect Level

LUBRICATION

Don't forget to grease any grease fittings, (also known as zerks, or alemites). Believe it or not synthetic grease is available for this purpose. This same grease is also used for wheel bearings, universal joints, ETC., some cars (and trucks) have grease fittings, others do not. Many vehicles have what is called a constant velocity joint (C.V. joint or joints). These usually run a long time. Failure usually comes from abuse or damage resulting when the C.V. joint 'boot' fails allowing grease out and dirt in. All front wheel drive cars have C.V. joints and some 4X4 trucks have them as well, in both cases just inside the front wheel hubs. C.V. joints, when repaired or serviced, usually require a special grease and are usually best to be dealt with by a professional. This would be a good time to visually inspect the tires. Problems here can crop up un-announced and needless to say tires are way too critical to ignore. I strongly recommend keeping tires properly inflated at all times. Not only does this prolong the life of the tire, but results in a vehicle that handles better and gets better fuel economy due to a decreased rolling resistance. Radial tires offer less rolling resistance than bias-ply tires, by the way.

BRAKES

With all this go you gotta have some whoa! Brakes, unfortunately, are usually neglected. The average man or woman in the street is not skilled in the inspection or repair of brakes. But as a driver of the vehicle, nobody knows better than you when something starts to feel funny-brakes included. If in doubt-check 'em out. Better sooner than later.

How do you know when your shocks or struts are going bad? Usually if your vehicle continues to bounce after you hit a bump. If you see oil leaking from your shocks or struts-they have seen their better days!

Another thing I recommend that is frequently overlooked is to do a walk around and check all lights and blinkers. Have a friend press the brake pedal to check for properly operating brake lights. Not only is this a good idea for safety, it could keep you from having an unwanted conservation with a police officer!

ADDITIVES

How about those additives? Now here is a hotly debated, frequently discussed subject. We've all seen the commercials on T.V. Some of them make some pretty outlandish claims. I am not about to get in the middle of this debate, but I do have an opinion. The only additive I have ever used is one that thickens the oil for use in a smoking knocking old engine. In this case it is at best a stop gap measure. As for the other additives I wont pass judgement on them. In my personal vehicles I keep the engine and gearboxes full of clean synthetic lubricants and that is it. These vehicles are doing fine, Thank You! To be sure some of these additives may be just as wonderful as their maker claims. Go with your heart on this one.

I hope I have helped you in some way with the information in this manual. Maybe I have answered a question, or perhaps I have encouraged you to ask new questions the answer to which might just benefit you. Perhaps now you are more aware of various aspects of your vehicle. Perhaps now you see your ride in a different light. They are pretty amazing aren't they? At any rate, thanks again for taking the time to purchase and review this manual. Most of all- BE CAREFUL OUT THERE!

P.S.

You may have noticed I didn't really get into the tune-up thing. I could write a separate manual on this subject, indeed many manuals have been written on this subject. Tune-ups are a part of routine maintenance and it is true that an improperly tuned engine frequently dirties up its oil faster. So yes, it is desirable to keep an engine properly tuned, not only for better performance and fuel economy but to allow the oil to better do its job.

NOTES

NOTES

NOTES

NOTES

NOTES

NOTES

NOTES

NOTES

NOTES

NOTES

Printed in the United States
874900001B